Conspiracy Theories

The Controversial Stories, Deception And Beliefs Of Our Worlds Most Mystifying Conspiracy Theories

Conspiracy Theories

© **Copyright 2015 by Seth Balfour - All rights reserved.**

This document is geared towards providing exact and reliable information in regards to the topic and issue covered. The publication is sold with the idea that the publisher is not required to render accounting, officially permitted, or otherwise, qualified services. If advice is necessary, legal or professional, a practiced individual in the profession should be ordered.

- From a Declaration of Principles which was accepted and approved equally by a Committee of the American Bar Association and a Committee of Publishers and Associations.

In no way is it legal to reproduce, duplicate, or transmit any part of this document in either electronic means or in printed format. Recording of this publication is strictly prohibited and any storage of this document is not allowed unless with written permission from the publisher. All rights reserved.

The information provided herein is stated to be truthful

and consistent, in that any liability, in terms of inattention or otherwise, by any usage or abuse of any policies, processes, or directions contained within is the solitary and utter responsibility of the recipient reader. Under no circumstances will any legal responsibility or blame be held against the publisher for any reparation, damages, or monetary loss due to the information herein, either directly or indirectly.

Respective authors own all copyrights not held by the publisher.

The information herein is offered for informational purposes solely, and is universal as so. The presentation of the information is without contract or any type of guarantee assurance.

The trademarks that are used are without any consent, and the publication of the trademark is without permission or backing by the trademark owner. All trademarks and brands within this book are for clarifying purposes only and are the owned by the owners themselves, not affiliated with this document.

Cover image courtesy of Ingrid Taylar – Flickr - https://www.flickr.com/photos/taylar/5542354448/

Conspiracy Theories

Table of Contents

Introduction	vi
Chapter 1: Types of Conspiracies	1
Chapter 2: The Moon Landing	3
Chapter 3: The Bermuda Triangle	7
Chapter 4: The Yeti	16
Chapter 5: Elvis	20
Chapter 6: Princess Diana	23
Chapter 7: Osama Bin Laden	28
Chapter 8: Political Cover-ups	36
Conclusion	43
Check Out My Other Books	44
Want more books?	46

Want more books?

Would you love books delivered straight to your inbox every week?

Free?

How about non-fiction books on all kinds of subjects?

We send out e-books to our loyal subscribers every week to download and enjoy!

All you have to do is join! It's so easy!

Just visit the link at the end of this book to sign up and then wait for your books to arrive!

Introduction

I want to thank you and congratulate you for purchasing the book, "Conspiracy Theories: *The Controversial Stories, Deception and Beliefs of Our Worlds Most Mystifying Conspiracy Theories*".

Conspiracy theories have always been able to pique interest among the old and young alike. Unbelievable tales and plans that allegedly took immense planning and impeccable execution have always remained all-time favourites. This book aims to bring to you some of the biggest conspiracy theories ever recorded.

From the moon landing to the Bermuda triangle, there are many alleged conspiracy theories right under our noses. Ultimately, most conspiracy theories may seem like oversold fiction due to a lack of evidence for supporting the theory.

The words "conspiracy theory" had originally been a neutral term. Since the assassination of U.S. president, John F. Kennedy it has taken a derogatory meaning. Nowadays, conspiracy theories are seen as elaborate cover ups put in place by malevolent intelligence agencies in the best interests of their country's political stance and/or to hide their own mishaps.

It can be defined as an elaborate explanation that openly accuses two or more persons, a group or an organization of having been the root cause or for covering up through premeditated action and secret conspiracy, an illegal or harmful event that may have resulted in possible death or crisis.

Thanks again for purchasing this book, I hope you enjoy it!

Chapter 1:
Types of Conspiracies

Conspiracy theories aren't something entirely new. It has been around for centuries. A careful assessment of all the conspiracy theories publicized so far reveals some distinct differences between each theory. Author, Jesse Walker has been able to compile conspiracy theories into five distinct types.

- Enemy outside – This type portrays malevolent figures mobilizing outside the community to scheme against it.

- Enemy within – In this case, the conspirators are most likely to be found within the community and have usually blended in with the ordinary citizens. A good example for this type would be sleeper cells.

- Enemy above – This is the most common type of conspiracy theory. The people in power, the "big-shots" of the community manipulate the system for their own profit, usually a position of importance or unparalleled power.

- Enemies below – There have been cases in the past where the lower working class have gone out of their way to effectively put an end to a dictatorship or a monarchy. These are just examples. In this type of conspiracy theory, the lower class people introduce anarchy into a well-defined system to overthrow or bring a government to its knees. These conspiracies are very blatant and hard to ignore because of the sheer number of people involved.

- Benevolent conspiracies - These type of conspiracies are usually the most controversial. They are highly secretive and very well planned and executed. Usually, the public is made aware of these conspiracy theories decades after it actually happened. Unlike terrorists or other malicious workers who take credit for any confusion caused no matter how slight, this type usually has a good intention/motive. Most such conspiracies are well guarded secrets. A good example would be the movements made by groups like the Freemasons.

Chapter 2:

The Moon Landing

Ever since man was able to conceive the idea of making his mark on the moon, work began in earnest to see who would succeed in making the first mark on the lunar surface. Developing countries and super power nations alike began contributing huge amounts of money solely towards the development space travel and manned lunar landings. It became a rage across the world and spread like cancer.

Immediately after the Second World War, the Soviets and U.S became established as super powers; two countries that had the power to change the course of the future. In 1957, Willey Ley (Spaceflight advocate, German-American science writer and historian of science who helped commercialize space travel and natural history in both Germany and the United States) wrote that it was possible to manufacture a rocket towards the end of the year, if somebody was found to sign the concerned papers. That statement made waves.

Conspiracy Theories

On Oct 4th 1957, the *Sputnik 1* was launched by the Soviet Union. It was the very first unmanned satellite that orbited the earth. It effectively flagged off the Space Race. The U.S responded to this show of power vigorously by greatly accelerating their military space projects by creating a civilian space agency, what we know as NASA.

Conspiracy theories start from the early Soviet unscrewed lunar missions. Instead of naming each launch attempt beforehand, the Soviets assigned a "Luna" mission a number only if the launch managed to get the spacecraft going beyond the earth's orbit.

This was done to hide from public view the number of failed attempts that lead up to each successful launch. Furthermore, if the launch succeeded in making it to the earth's orbit but failed before departing for the moon, it was assigned a "Sputnik" or "Cosmos" number to mask it as an Earth orbit mission, thus hiding its true purpose. They also took great care to ensure that launch explosions were not accounted for at all.

The potential conspiracy theories that took centre stage during the Space Race was the claim that said some or all elements that were related to the Apollo program were elaborate hoaxes staged by NASA with the aid of

Conspiracy Theories

supporting organizations.

The most notable and outright claim is that the six crewed or manned landings that took place between 1969-1972 we elaborately faked and not even one of the twelve Apollo astronauts ever actually walked on the moon. During the mid-1970 period there has been great activity that claims that the manned landings were a hoax.

Conspiracy theorists or "conspiracists" led the public to believe that NASA and similar organizations have been leading on the general public with claims about manned landings. These groups have sometimes gone so far to stress their point that they have been accused of manufacturing, destroying and tampering with evidence. The evidence included photos, radio transmissions, TV transmissions and telemetry tapes. Some accusations have gone so far as to accuse the conspiracy theorists of trying to subdue key witnesses.

The origins of these theories can be traced back to a book; *'We Never Went to the Moon: America's Thirty Billion Dollar Swindle'* published in 1976 by Bill Kaysing. Kaysing worked as a senior technical writer in Rocketdyne (company that built the F-1 engines used on the Saturn V rocket), although, he had no knowledge of either technical writing or rocket engines.

His book made many allegations, including one that claimed the probability of a successful manned landing was only 0.0017%. He also claimed that despite close monitoring by the USSR, it would have been immensely easier for NASA to fake the moon landings than to actually go there.

Countering these accusations NASA has been able to clarify the matter to some extent although some finer points are left open to debate. In the beginning of the 21st century, LROs (Lunar Reconnaissance Orbiter) have been able to capture high resolution images of lander modules and the tracks left by the astronauts. The deciding factor came in 2012 when NASA released an image that showed five out of six Apollo missions' flags erected on the moon still standing (Apollo 11's flag was knocked down by the takeoff rocket's exhaust. The flag still remains.).

Even then, conspiracy theorists managed to manipulate public interest for more than 40 years at a stretch. Even now, there are speculations about the first landing being faked in 1969 just to win the Space Race.

Chapter 3:

The Bermuda Triangle

Somewhere, in a remote western part of the North Atlantic Ocean, there have been numerous reports of aircrafts and seaworthy vessels disappearing under extremely mysterious circumstances. The Unites States Navy refuses to acknowledge the existence of such an area and maintains no record of it on the U.S board of geographic names. Due to this refusal, there is no well-defined area for the Bermuda Triangle.

The area and boundaries of the triangle are subject to change depending on which writer chooses to report the incident. The most popular and publicly accepted vertices of the Bermuda Triangle are Miami, Florida peninsula, San Juan, Puerto Rico and in the mid-Atlantic island of Bermuda. Subsequent writers haven't strictly stuck to this definition and so the area of the triangle has been known to vary from 500,000 to 1, 510,000 square miles.

Until now, the triangle has been held responsible for the alleged disappearance of over 2000 ships and 75 aircraft which have vanished from the face of the earth without leaving any trace.

The earliest recorded documentation of the anomalous behavior surrounding the Bermuda Triangle was put forth by Christopher Columbus in 1492. He claimed to have seen strange dancing lights and flames in the sky. He also reported bizarre compass readings in that area.

After Columbus put the New World on the map, many countries sent out galleons and ships to explore it. However, a lot of these vessels had sunk without any trace under mysterious circumstances. Although modern salvaging equipment has succeeded in discovering wrecks from that period, they haven't been able to determine with certainty how they sank.

Most notable incidents involving the Bermuda Triangle

Ellen Austin and the prize crew

During early sailing days, if a crew managed to defeat the enemy then it could take over the enemy's ship. Keeping

Conspiracy Theories

such a situation in mind, most warships carried extra crew members to be posted on an enemy ship if they were to defeat one. These extra crew members were called a "prize crew".

They had the responsibility of claiming the prize and bringing it back to the port where they would be assigned the vessel if they were found worthy of it, after a trial. In 1881, *Ellen Austin* chanced upon an abandoned ship and posted a prize crew on board. They intended to sail it to New York.

According to history, the ship went missing. Conspiracy theorists say that the ship later reappeared without the prize crew. Some conspiracy theorists have gone so far as to say that the ship disappeared once again with an alternate prize crew on board.

Hard evidence is able to back the fact that there existed an *Ellen Austin* at that time. However, there has been no evidence of any casualty on board. Especially, any casualty suggesting that a prize crew disappeared.

USS Cyclops

One of the recorded accidents surrounding the Bermuda

Conspiracy Theories

Triangle that had a large death toll and the single largest death toll under unnatural circumstances in the glorious history of the American Navy happened aboard the Navy vessel USS *Cyclops*.

Around the 4th of March, 1918 the USS *Cyclops* departed from the island of Barbados. The collier was laden with a full load of manganese ore. It was also handicapped as one of its engines was not in working order. The entire ship, its crew and the cargo disappeared without a trace. Multiple theories exist, attempting to explain the loss of the ship.

The most common reasons include capsizing and under the radar wartime activity. The best logical argument put forward to counter this conspiracy theory was that the ship sank because of structural failure. The collier was not designed to carry that kind of weight, so there is a good chance that it might have capsized in choppy waters.

There has been intense speculation on this topic because it seemed that such a large ship with such an obvious cargo couldn't disappear without the slightest trace. Also, this incident resulted in the most lives ever lost by the US Navy. A grand total of 309 crew members were lost in this incident.

Carroll A. Deering

The *Carroll Deering* was a five-mast schooner built in 1919. On the 31st of January, 1921 she was discovered abandoned and hard aground at Diamond Shoals, near Cape Hatteras, North Carolina. This case wasn't scrutinized much because she was suspected of illegal rum-running. Another ship, *SS Hewitt* went missing roughly around the same timeline and is rumoured to be involved in the *Carroll Deering* incident.

Flight 19

On the 5th of December, 1945, 5 TBM torpedo bombers went missing during a training exercise. The squadron had received orders to return to base at the end of the exercise. The whole squadron was never heard from again. This incident went on to amplify whatever belief people had about supernatural occurrences in the Bermuda triangle.

The only explanation offered by the military base was that the aircraft could have experienced a navigational error

Conspiracy Theories

and eventually run out of fuel. This incident became more controversial when a search and rescue mission set out to look for them. PBM Mainer had a 13-man crew on board at the time. However, she also went missing. There have been reports where a tanker off the coast of Florida reported to have seen an explosion but no survivors were found.

Star Tiger and Star Ariel

Star Tiger, on a flight from Azores to Bermuda on the 30th of January 1948, disappeared without a trace. A year later the *Star Ariel* disappeared on January 17, 1949, when flying from Bermuda to Kingston, Jamaica. Both these aircraft were commissioned by the British South American Airways. Later, it was claimed that these planes were barely fit for flight and it wouldn't have been a surprise that they may have crashed.

Douglas DC-3

Plane number NC16002 (a Douglas DC-3 aircraft) vanished on the 28th of December, 1948, when making a run from San Juan, Puerto Rico, to Miami. It vanished without a trace, taking along with it 32 people on board.

Documentation revealed that the plane was ordered to fly even when inspection revealed that it was low on battery. However, there has been much speculation over this as the plane's engine wasn't dependent on batteries. So, this theory is not very strongly convincing.

KC-135 Stratotankers

Another highly hyped accident concerning the Triangle involved a couple of US Air Force KC-135 Stratotanker. The Triangle inspired version states that both the aircraft did collide but there were two individual crash sites, at a distance of 260km from each other. However, a search and rescue ship investigated the site and found that the second site was faked. All it contained was a collection of driftwood and seaweed tangled in an old buoy.

Connemara IV

The *Connemara IV* was a pleasure yacht. It was found adrift in the south of Bermuda on September 1955. The Triangle conspiracy stated that the crew on board had gone missing and the yacht was found adrift under mysterious circumstances. Further investigation uncovered that she had broken off and dragged her moorings out to sea.

There have been many allegations and explanations trying to make sense of the various mysterious happenings. Some of the most popular explanations have put forth alleged paranormal or extra-terrestrial involvement. Formally documented evidence says that a notable percentage of the accusations made concerning the Bermuda Triangle are spurious or blown out of proportion by writers and movie makers.

In 2013, the World Wide Fund for Nature took a survey identifying the world's most dangerous waters for shipping but surprisingly, the Bermuda Triangle was not among them.

Supernatural musings

The suspense and controversy surrounding the Bermuda Triangle has subjected it to be the target for a lot of super natural accusations. The most popular was the alleged presence of the Lost City of Atlantis in the vicinity. Film-makers have popularized an element of extra-terrestrial involvement too. The victims of the lost Flight 19 incident have been publicized as alien abductees.

Natural explanations

Conspiracy Theories

- Magnetic anomalies
- Heavy surface currents
- Human error
- Unpredictable and violent weather
- Methane hydrates

Chapter 4:
The Yeti

It is safe to assume that there isn't a person on the planet who hasn't heard of the yeti, in one form or another. Although, the elusive snowman keeps strictly to himself, he has managed to garner more attention than your average attention-seeking pop star. Through cartoons, journals and other media the abominable snowman has managed to strike fear or curiosity into the hearts of people across the globe.

The Yeti is an ape like being that is said to inhabit the Himalayan region of Nepal and Tibet. It is an extremely elusive being and there is no proper picture yet to prove its existence. There have been fleeting glimpses and occasional glimpses. These sightings have been so varied and far apart (with respect to time) that it has raised questions about the existence of a whole species.

The most popular myth would be that we have been sighting the same abominable snowman over the years. The names Yeti and Meh-Teh are the names that the

Conspiracy Theories

abominable snowman is known by the most.

The Yeti was an integral part of pre-Buddhist beliefs. Records show that the Lepcha people considered it a deity. It was worshipped as a God of the Hunt mostly referred to as the "Glacier Being". During the mid-nineteenth century, sightings of the Yeti increased but were dismissed as mountain animals. From the beginning of the twentieth century there has been an increase in the number of westerners to visit the country, with the sole purpose of sighting or capturing the elusive snowman.

Since then, there have been increases in the number of claims at sighting the Yeti. It was around this time that the famous Yeti hoax came into existence. It went viral and came to be popularly known as the *Snow Walker Film*.

As opposed to common knowledge, physical evidence of the Yeti does exist. However, the way in which the tests and other studies done on the specimen was not very ethical. In Khumjung village, Pangboche, Nepal there exists a monastery that claimed to have a hand and scalp form the Yeti.

When this discovery was made in the modern age, oil

businessman and adventurer Tom slick led an expedition to acquire photographs of the artefact and possible persuade them to give it up for detailed analysis. His team was able to acquire photographs but was unable to retrieve the hand for examination.

A man called Peter Byrne, from Slick's team managed to acquire a few bones from the hand in 1959. Peter Byrne was allowed to examine the hand but was not permitted to take it away for examination. So he removed a few bones from the hand and replaced it with human counterparts that he had managed to sneak into the compound.

Later, he re-wrapped the hand to hide his theft. Byrne managed to circumvent security and smuggled the items into India. Smuggling the bones out of India was an entirely different matter. There are rumors which say that he allegedly sought the help of well-known Hollywood actor, James Stewart. Allegedly, Mr. Stewart and his wife helped Byrne to smuggle it out of the country by hiding it in his luggage.

The specimens were submitted to prominent primatologist from London University, William Osman Hill. He ran a physical examination on the pieces. The first results declared that the samples were only human. On further scrutiny, he decided that the pieces had more in common with a Neanderthal than a *homo sapien.*

It was then subjected to a more detailed and intensive tissue analysis. After careful examination, it was determined that the tissue was definitely not human. They could only verify that it was "near human".

In the coming years these findings were called a bluff. The fact that the specimens were stolen and disappeared into a private collection did not help matters. A report that said that the DNA was definitely human, simply added fuel to the fire. Regardless of what conspiracy theorists might instigate, the presence of physical evidence was often considered ultimate in all debates that rose on the subject.

Chapter 5:

Elvis

This man is more commonly known as "The King", than by his real name. The real man behind this globally known façade was called Elvis Aaron Presley. He is without doubt the most iconic man to have lived in the twentieth century. He was born into a family in Tupelo, Mississippi. He relocated to Memphis, Tennessee at the age of 13 where his music career took off in 1954. His first single, *Heartbreak Hotel* earned him fame across the United States.

As in real life, the King managed to stir up a lot of controversy in the afterlife too. The conspiracy theory that claims he faked his death is still ubiquitous and a topic that has always seen heated discussion. On August 16, 1977 The King was found lifeless on the bathroom floor of his suite.

A team of paramedics was called in. when they failed to revive him, he was rushed to the Baptist Memorial hospital. Thirty minutes later they declared that the most

Conspiracy Theories

iconic personality of the twentieth century was no more.

The post mortem reported that cardiac arrest and heart disease was the most probable cause behind his death. The following years saw a rise in the number of insinuated conspiracy theories against Elvis' death. One argument went on about the alive vs. dead debate and faked death vs. actual death. Another set of people focused mainly on the death being a cardiac arrest or a drug overdose.

The people who claim that his death was faked have based their accusations on the following

- A spelling mistake on the gravestone
- Alleged sightings of The King himself
- An unclaimed insurance policy
- Alleged body replacement
- Need to "disappear"
- Possible victim under witness protection

Although most of these reasons lack any solid evidence to see them through, one reason stands out. The unclaimed insurance policy has raised quite a stir. Especially after lawyers pointed out that collecting the policy when the policy holder is still alive is illegal. The continued neglect

Conspiracy Theories

on the Presley estate's behalf at collecting the money has raised suspicions, questioning the facts.

There are no facts to support the theory that Elvis faked his death, and the debate itself is not valid. It is time to set the record straight and properly frame the issue because this faulty debate has gone on far too long. Many Elvis fans are tired of it, the tabloids seem to have become tired of it, and certainly the Presley family has heard enough about it.

Chapter 6:

Princess Diana

When you hear the word princess, after Cinderella and Jasmine, the first name that comes to your mind would be Diana. She was born as the fourth child into the aristocratic family of John Spencer and Frances Ruth Roche. She was born on the 1st of July 1961. She acquired worldwide fame when she got engaged to Charles, the Prince of Wales, who was the heir to Queen Elizabeth the Second.

Their globally celebrated wedding took place on the 29th of July 1981 at St. Paul's cathedral. Popularly known as Princess Diana, she also bore the titles of Princess of Wales, Duchess of Rothesay, Duchess of Cornwall, Baroness of Renfrew and Countess of Chester.

She actively headed a lot of international charities and did some amazing fund raising work. Her untimely demise was mourned by her fans all over the world. Her road accident also claimed the lives of two other people who were travelling with her; Dodi Fayed and Henri Paul.

Conspiracy Theories

Fayed was the son of Egyptian billionaire Al-Fayed. He was a known friend and associate of Princess Diana. Henri Paul was the acting security manager of the Hotel Ritz, Paris.

The circumstance of her death and the events that led up to it weren't very convincing to the public eye. This generated a lot of conspiracy theories about her death and whether her car accident was really an accident. The crash occurred just after midnight on the 31st of august, 1997. Some of the much hyped theories around this mystery are discussed below.

Initially, the French investigation declared that the accident was indeed just what it claimed to be; an accident. In a conclusion to that report, they declared that it was caused due to the driver, Henri Paul who was allegedly drunk behind the wheel.

An inquest initiated in London came to an end in 2008, declaring that the accident was caused purely due to negligence on the driver's side. They also mentioned that, the driver may have driven that rashly to evade the pursuing paparazzi.

A very interesting theory to the whole affair states that the

Conspiracy Theories

Princess had tried to fake her own death but then the plan had gone horribly wrong. It caught everyone's attention that Dodi's usual driver wasn't used. It is said that Paul had stepped in at the last minute to drive the car. Later investigation revealed that none of the hotel employees knew much about him. He was described as a quiet man who kept to himself.

Theories instigate that he was in on the plan and was in cahoots with the Al-Fayed family. Cause for suspicion was provided when it took almost two full days for his name to be revealed.

Another interesting fact that supports this theory was that Princess Diana had let slip to reporter Richard Kray that she intended to wholly withdraw from public life. This theory didn't quite take off among radical tinkers because it was inconceivable that Diana would abandon her children.

Another plot declares that the MI6 took out Princess Diana. This theory accuses the MI6 of having a very paranoid perspective on threats. It says that the MI6 might have found Princess Diana to be a threat who was capable of causing national unrest with her words or actions. The alleged involvement of the MI6 during the leakage of the phone tapping tapes that put Diana in a bad light was quite enough for almost sealing the accusation.

A quick investigation into bodyguard Trevor Rees-Jones reveals that he was a former member of the crack Parachute Regiment, one of the toughest in the British army. He also completed two stints in Northern Ireland and served in the Royal Military Police, just the kind of background that would have seen him come into contact with members of the secret service.

The fact that he survived the whole nasty affair makes theorists believe he was in with MI6 on the whole plan. This theory also doesn't appeal to a logical mind mainly because its motives lack promise.

A plausible theory that could be capable of explaining the whole affair would be that the actual target was not Princess Diana at all. It seems that public speculation hasn't considered that the son of billionaire Fayed could have been the real target. As a very wealthy man with a history of questionable dealings it is only natural that he might have made a few enemies on the way.

This plot could have been designed to take out Dodi Fayed using Diana as a cover up to take attention away from the

Conspiracy Theories

real target. Or Princess Diana could have ended up as collateral damage, being in the wrong place at the wrong time. This theory didn't gain momentum because not many people were ready to believe that any assassin would use someone as famous as Diana for a cover up. When it was obvious that any accident involving her would be well looked into.

Mohammed Al-Fayed, owner of the Paris Ritz publicly stated that it was no accident and openly pointed fingers at the MI6 and the Duke of Edinburgh. Although after the final hearing in 2008, he dropped charges.

Chapter 7:

Osama Bin Laden

The man who was known for the people he murdered than those he lived for. Osama bin Mohammed bin Awad bin Laden; he was born into the household of billionaire business Mohammed bin Awad bin Laden. Although no records exist to support it, it has been accepted that his birthday is on the 10th of March, 1957.

He was the beloved son of a wealthy construction magnate, a family that had close relations with the Royal family of Saudi. His student life remains a mystery.

Some reports claim that he was a stellar student with a degree in civil engineering and public administration to his name. Other stories claim that he dropped out of college in his third year. He was a shrewd man, of which we have no doubt. During his tenure at the university, he did show an avid interest in religion and took a lot of interest in translating the Holy books.

After 1979, Laden left college and joined hands with

Abdullah Azzam to support the Soviet war for the mujahideen resistance in Afghanistan. In 1988, he split ways with Azzam and founded the al-Qaeda. From then on, his life has been infamous. On May 2, 2011, he was gunned to death by U.S forces. The following are some of the conspiracy theories surrounding his life and death.

Osama was not a part of the 9/11 attacks

Following the 9/11 attacks, Osama Bin Laden made a public statement, his exact words were;

"I was not involved in the September 11 attacks in the United States nor did I have knowledge of the attacks. There exists a government within a government within the United States. The United States should try to trace the perpetrators of these attacks within itself; to the people who want to make the present century a century of conflict between Islam and Christianity. That secret government must be asked as to who carried out the attacks."

Furthermore, there have been claims that Osama Bin Laden has been allegedly dead since at least 2003. And that the United States did not kill the real Osama bin Laden on May 1st. It has been suggested that the decision

Conspiracy Theories

to bury Osama at sea is mainly to cover up this fact. Any examination could have revealed the truth. This evidently draws the summary that he was not a willing player and that he had not foretold information of the conspired attacks of 9/11.

If he was as guilty as accused, he would surely have had at least an idea about when the attacks were to happen even if he hadn't been informed about the exact date. Then it is safe to assume that he would not have put himself in danger of being captured or killed.

Yet, he did do some seemingly daring actions that he showcased. These facts are supported by some of the bold and mind boggling actions he took. In the month of July 2001, he admitted himself into a hospital in Dubai and stayed for more than a week. During this time he was visited by a CIA officer.

On September 10, 2001, he willingly sought medical aid at a hospital located near the border of Pakistan and Afghanistan. It seems highly illogical that a person with such a history of crime would be so outright in his dealings. This jaywalking attitude of his raised many questions about his alleged involvement in the terror attacks.

Some people call him, the original Boogie man. He is said to have pulled the strings behind this whole fiasco. In reality, the United States is trying to keep this man in the limelight to perpetuate its malicious intents. Adding to this confusion, there have been various reports by Osama experts claiming that many of the photos released by the U.S are fake. In fact, the video tape that got released after 9/11 has been claimed to be counterfeit.

Osama has been dead for at least a decade

This controversial accusation states that the real Osama died as early as 2002. It accuses the United States of keeping him alive so that they would get a free license to barge into any country that they may want a look into. If questioned, they had the license to flash a "pursuing international criminal" badge. A job that might have been a tedious affair could now be done right in the open in the name of trying to capture a most wanted terrorist.

This theory has struck radical thinkers as being extremely plausible as the U.S military movements across the Middle East is a well-known fact. Another strange thing that doesn't add up is how the authorities managed to collect details of the hijackers from the 9/11 attacks on such short notice.

There have been rumors which state that none of those attackers died in the incident and that has managed to create a few intriguing conspiracy theories in its own right. What left the audience baffled in this incident was that none of the names of the people involved or any of their known aliases were found on the flight list of the planes involved in the crash.

Osama was an undercover CIA asset?

Journalist James Corbett said of Bin Laden's death as a "retirement party for an old CIA asset, along the lines of Lee Harvey Oswald in 1963." Mr. Corbett insists that Osama was a valuable CIA asset and his sole intention was to be made the scapegoat of the 9/11 attacks to mask the incompetence of the intelligence agencies at finding the real perpetrators. Javad Jahangirzadeh, the Iranian security official had something to say along the same lines, he insinuated that Osama was a part of a US plot to defame Islam and create an aggressive image in its place. Once he had served his purpose, he was eliminated.

The new videos are CIA fakes

This would be a more digestible theory, for the people who believe that bin Laden is not alive and the U.S. government is masterminding a vast fraud. This accusation isn't something new and has been discussed back and forth for years. Different people give versatile reasons, why the American President would open his trump card at this stage, a few months prior to the elections.

There are some who say it was to bolster his frail ratings; others say that it was a ruse to take away attention from the birth certificate scandal. Heidar Moslehi, Iran's intelligence minister said Laden had been dead for a few years now and maintained that Laden's killing was in fact a hoax which was meant to divert people from the Islamic awakening.

Kevin Lake, at the Free Patriot had received a letter from his friend in the US Special forces. The letter is as follows;

"I'll tell you something you that will make you think…Did you ever ask yourself why our Government never showed (undeniable) proof of the dead body of Osama Bin Laden. And why nearly the whole SEAL TEAM SIX got killed in strange circumstances? Helicopter crashes, parachute accidents etc. Well, I have a friend in that team who told me that they never made a capture of Bin Laden...it was a setup from Obama to get elected again as President. No Sailor or Soldier had ever seen the funeral or the dead body of Bin Laden on board the aircraft carrier. People say that Osama died years ago in a Drone strike... and Navy Seals are not allowed to give any information about that mission where Bin Laden was captured. We believe our Government- everything they tell to us- like dumb sheep. They manipulate us with the media which is also working for the government. America is dying step by step, because of stupid people who still believe or support Obama. He is the modern Anti-Christ, who will lead us into a 3rd World War! It´s just a question of time...you will see! Bin Laden is a lie, his death is a lie and the guy was a boogey man created by the CIA years ago. I'm beginning to think that the theory that jihadists are all CIA created to make Islam look bad, to create a new bogeyman after the fall of communism to keep their fascist plans in place and rolling."

Osama was betrayed by his right hand man

There have been speculations that Al-Qaida's next in line,

Ayman al-Zawahiri, gave away the whereabouts of Laden to the US to strategically position the terrorist organization under Egyptian control. Egyptians have wanted control over the organization since its inception; they saw they had their best chance in mid-2004 when Osama fell ill. Then Zawahiri convinced Laden to relocate to Abbottabad. Bin Laden was alive and being held in a secret location while the US interrogated him about al-Qaida's nuclear arsenal.

The Illuminati effect

The deaths of Laden and Hitler were reported on 1st of May. This has raised some eyebrows regarding the involvement of the elite group, Illuminati. The coincidence that May 1st also happens to be their second most important holiday is worth a thought or two.

Chapter 8:

Political Cover-ups

Politics, since time immemorial has been identical to a game of chess. Where the strength of each move you make is dependent on the timing. I wouldn't go as far as to call politics a game of lies or a blurred bureaucracy. Then it always had its own secrets.

Blatant lies have been spread to gain political progress or a foothold over a rival political body. Sometimes, parts of the truth have been hidden and have proved to be more fatal as compared to lying about it. As a political party or movement, publicity is paramount and almost a mantra for them.

Although politicians argue that any publicity is good publicity, to lose face would mean equally devastating results during a poll. A politician is only as successful as his P.R team makes him.

In spite of all this, politicians have been known to be involved in scams, sexual harassment, smuggling, treason, etc. the media hounds have sincerely reported everything they could get their hands on. However, some shocking stories have been reported and lost to the wind due to a lack of evidence. These priceless and sometimes horrific accounts have taken to haunting blogs and dinner conversations as conspiracy theories.

Let us take a glance at a few conspiracy theories that have been claimed to be huge political cover ups.

ISIS

We all know ISIS as an extremist terrorist organization that has a base of operations in and around the Middle East region. ISIS stands for Islamic State of Iraq and Syria. Their involvement includes but is not limited to events like the Iraq War (2003-2011), Syrian War, Second Libyan War, the Sinai insurgency and War in Afghanistan (present day).

They are infamous for everything from child soldiers to the ill treatment and sexual harassment of the women in ISIS controlled areas. Recently, they have made waves by executing journalists. Following Osama's death, there rose conspiracy theories that stated that he was a U.S puppet, created with the sole purpose of allowing U.S to

Conspiracy Theories

monitor the Middle East.

These conspiracies added fuel to the accusations and rumors existing around ISIS. Conspiracy theories began to crop up stating that ISIS was a front created by the U.S in close association with Israel. This theory holds possible room for debate, as these two countries stand to gain the most from the overthrowing of the Assad government of Syria.

NSA spying on commoners

The National Security Agency is the US government agency responsible for electronic surveillance. The NSA was accused of performing an almost impossible task. Spying on the personal communications of the American citizens! Later, the NSA have confessed to making use of a backdoor in surveillance law to conduct warrantless searches on American's communications.

The infamous PRISM program has some big names like Google, Facebook, YouTube, Skype etc. as participants. This program enables the NSA to get hold of personal information with ease. At first, the NSA denied any truth about the PRISM program. Gradually, it was forced to accept that PRISM was fully operational and in use.

Hitler

Over the years man has strived to expand his territories and for this cause wars have been won and lost, blood has been shed, friends have turned into foes, many a leader have walked this road and won battles some worth praise and others so horrifying that generations haven't forgotten about the horrors and brutality of it to this very day. One of the most notable leaders whose name is synonymous to the gruesome extent to which man can treat his fellow being without even a morsel of humanity was Adolf Hitler.

The cold blooded soulless murder of thousands and unspeakable acts of violence against the innocent, perpetuating fear and panic in people all over the world took place under his reign of terror. He was founder and leader of the Nazi party. He was born on 20th April 1889 as the fourth of 6 kids of Alois Hitler and his wife Klara Polzl.

As a child he was of a calm demeanour often partaking in church activities and even considered becoming a priest, but the death of his little brother Edmund brought on a change for the worse, he transformed from an outgoing and confident child to a reserved and sullen boy who picked fights with his superiors and after the demise of his father, Hitler who was enamoured by the German nationalist ideas, so he went off to pursue his dreams.

On the 30th of April, 1945 Hitler committed suicide when the war was lost and the Soviet army troops were a block away from the Reich Chancellery. His new wife, Eva Braun bit a Cyanide capsule while Hitler shot himself. Or so the world believed until conspiracy theories cropped up claiming Hitler's death was staged and that he lived on to the age of 95.

Recent declassified documents from the FBI that have seen the light mention the government was aware that Hitler and Eva Braun were well and alive, and lived at the foothills of the Andes Mountains, much after the 2nd World War. On the 30th of April 1945, Hitler allegedly killed himself in his private underground bunker.

His dead body was discovered and identified and then rushed to Russia by the Soviets. It may be indeed a fact that one of the most hated man (probably the most) in history, got away from Germany. He rather, lived a peaceful and leisurely life in the picturesque locales of the

Conspiracy Theories

Andes. Some FBI documents, which were released recently, show that Hitler and Braun's suicide was faked and also the infamous pair might have had first person assistance from Allan Dulles himself.

As per a FBI document published from Los Angles, the agency revealed that they were well aware and informed about an unknown submarine that made its way to the Argentine coast, and dropped off some high level Nazi officers. What is more jaw-dropping is they say that the FBI was aware that Hitler lived at the foothills of the Andes Mountains.

Even with perfect physical likeness and directions to their whereabouts, the FBI did not bother to follow up on this lead. Recovery of damning evidence, which placed the German submarine U-530 close to the Argentine coast did not inspire the FBI to investigate on the lead and perhaps expose one of the most intriguing conspiracy theories of the twentieth century.

In 1945, Washington got information from Buenos Aires which said that there is a great probability, as per which, Hitler and his new wife Eva Braun had moved to Argentina, which also coincided with sightings of the German submarine U-530. Later, Architect Alejandro

Conspiracy Theories

Bustillo wrote about the construction and designing of Hitler and Eva's new home that was allegedly financed by rich and powerful German immigrants.

Perhaps the most deciding factor that plays in favour of the conspiracy theory would be examination of Hitler's alleged remains. In 2009, an archaeologist, Nicholas Bellatoni was cleared for performing some DNA tests on a skull fragment that was recovered.

The DNA samples did not match those of Hitler. Neither were they a match for the familiar Eva Braun. This theory looks very promising and may shed some light on the mystery surrounding his death.

Conclusion

Thank you again for purchasing this book!

I hope this book was able to help you to address your curiosity regarding some of the biggest conspiracy theories from around the world. As interesting as they sound, there is a big cloud of inconsistency with most of these theories.

Nevertheless, these theories are extremely intriguing and interesting. I hope you had fun learning more about these theories.

If you liked this book, would you be kind enough to leave me a review on Amazon? Just search for this title and my name on Amazon to find it. Thank you very much, it is very much appreciated!

Check Out My Other Books

Below you'll find some of my other popular books that are popular on Amazon and Kindle as well. You can visit my author page on Amazon to see other work done by me. (Seth Balfour).

- **True Ghost Stories**
- **UFOs And Aliens**
- **Conspiracy Theories**
- **Missing People**
- **Serial Killers**
- **Cannibal Killers**
- **Missing People – Volume 2**
- **Unexplained Disappearances**
- **Cold Cases True Crime**
- **Haunted Asylums**
- **Haunted Asylums – Volume 2**

Conspiracy Theories

True Ghost Stories – Volume 2

Women Who Kill

If the links do not work, for whatever reason, you can simply search for these titles on the Amazon website with my name to find them.

Want more books?

Would you love books delivered straight to your inbox every week?

Free?

How about non-fiction books on all kinds of subjects?

We send out e-books to our loyal subscribers every week to download and enjoy!

All you have to do is join! It's so easy!

Just visit the link below to sign up and then wait for your books to arrive!

www.LibraryBugs.com

Enjoy :)

Printed in the USA
CPSIA information can be obtained
at www.ICGtesting.com
LVHW041143260524
781453LV00024B/306